With best wishes,

Aileen Hall

CANDLELIGHT

CANDLELIGHT

Poetry by

Aileen Hall

Exposition Press   Smithtown, New York

First Edition

© 1982 by Aileen Hall

ISBN 0-682-498106

Printed in the United States of America

To Walter, who gave me typewriters
and notebooks at Christmastime, and
who shared the candlelight

Contents

7

Foreword

If *Candelight* said no more (but it does) than the message in "The twig was shaped to be an upright tree," it is well worth the time it takes to share the world, the friends, the family, and the faith of Aileen Hall. In one short poem written to her child the reader will find the philosophy of the good life, the joy of parenthood, and the teachings of Jesus—a tall order for so few lines of verse, but she has somehow managed to capture them all.

There are other subjects about which the author's pen paints a most revealing and inspirational word portrait: "The Oak Tree"—her childish world of make-believe; "Prater Creek"—the playground of her youth; "The Quest We Shared"—her childhood friend who died; "I Married a Fisherman"—a not very subtle or unusual complaint of wives so afflicted; "Pop's House"—the never-ending, delightful story of grandparents and their grandchildren, and many other people, places, and events in her life . . . people, places, and events that we have all experienced and shared but never seemed to have the time or the talent to paint our own word picture as she has done for us.

The sincerity, honesty, forthrightness, and feelings—and the many other good characteristics of the author—are abundantly present in *Candlelight*. The reader will quickly come to this realization as Aileen Hall takes you on a word journey through life in rural Kentucky—life that she has experienced and expressed in her own inimitable style.

Finally, *Candlelight* is an expression of Aileen Hall's faith in God. A simple but profound faith that is best comprehended in the eight-line poem simply entitled "One Day" and used as part of the burial service for her father.

Having known the author for more years than either of us cares to acknowledge (vanity being what it is), it is difficult if not impossible to be objective about *Candlelight*. If I have failed to do so, I offer no apology. None is required. I simply recommend it for your reading pleasure and enjoyment.

EDWARD V. "PETE" DORSEY
Senior Assistant Postmaster General (Retired)

9

Candlelight

Whatever else a day may bring to me,
Of good or bad, of all that's wrong or right,
The evening is a special time to be
Bathed in the soft, warm glow of candlelight.

A dinner time with friends and family near,
With children's laughter sounding in the halls,
And I would have this favorite atmosphere
Enhanced by candle shadows on the walls.

At twilight time, I would have put away
The little cares I didn't want to know;
I'd take some time to see the children play,
To laugh and love and watch the candle-glow.

Garland

If I could take a vast array
    of words
And form them into just one
    small bouquet,
I'd want to use the softest
    ones I've heard
And weave them in some old
    familiar way.

I'd lay the boldest syllables
    aside
In preference for others,
    more subdued,
And when their pastel colors
    I had tried,
My bouquet would be soft and
    golden hued.

Then when you'd view my
    garland you would find
My stormy nature was denied
    a part,
And that its soft reflection
    had defined
The quiet peacefulness within
    my heart.

My Wish for You

It is not mine
    to give to you
Days of sunshine,
    skies of blue,
A path to lead
    where flowers grow,
Night with moonlight-
    starlight glow;

But if the days and
    weeks should bring
Not only these, but
    all good things,
Then my own happiness
    would be
As if they, too,
    were given me.

Sometime

I don't suppose there ever was
A time you lay awake,
Wishing I were there with you.
What difference would it make?

And probably you never came
Upon a view so grand
You wanted me to share it, too,
And maybe hold your hand.

I doubt that any banquet meal
For you was common fare
Because I dined a world away
When you would have me there;

But if sometime a quiet room,
Alight with candle-glow,
Should ever find you missing me,
Please, won't you tell me so?

Expect to go to Heaven looking back

The Common Trait

How many generations there have been
Between Lot's wife and me, I cannot tell;
The Sodom where she dwelt I've never seen,
Nor watched the fiery holocaust that fell.

But through the years, the trait that stopped her flight
Has come to me, though others I may lack;
And I hear there are those who think I might
Expect to go to Heaven looking back.

The Oak Tree

There is a stately, tall oak tree
That stands erect and loftily,
Reminding me of childish fun
Where we were shielded from the sun;
Where, with swings and scattered toys
And other barefoot girls and boys,
Our minds could easily conceive
The childish world of make-believe.

I reminisce of days we spent
Beneath this sturdy monument
To childish laughter, childish tears—
The memory of carefree years,
And wonder if a drooping bough
Can feel its age or if, somehow,
It's sad from being left alone
Since children, dolls and swings are gone.

Prater Creek

When I was a child, the world I knew
Was hill and valley, sky of blue.
For miles and miles a small stream wound
Through the lowest points of mountain ground,
And houses lined the land between
The mountainsides and valley stream.

From house to house the children played
And bare feet ran the paths they'd made
To the willow trees along the bank
Where pets and cows and horses drank;
And parents worked without a fear
For the stream was shallow, cool and clear.

When springtime rains fell on the land,
The creek bed filled and water ran
Across a cornfield's lowest reach
To leave behind a sandy beach
And the boys and girls would later tell
Of castle forms that rose and fell.

The children searched the stream and learned
Of the little curves where the water turned,
Creating depths they could behold
As a fishing spot or a swimming hole.
Then as the seasons changed they'd think
How the stream would freeze to a skating rink.

Now when my children ask of me,
"What was it like for a child to be
Without our modern recreation?"
I say, "Each day was like vacation,
And there's no joy a child could seek
More than we knew on Prater Creek."

Remembered Walk

The holiday is past but I recall
Our walk along the beach, with hand
    in hand,
The roaring of the waves that rise
    and fall,
And moonlight gleaming on the
    whitened sand.

I think about the stars, the clouds
    of white,
Like puffs of cotton floating on
    the air,
A gentle ocean breeze that brushed
    the night
And added to a magic atmosphere;

Our talk about the hopes and dreams
    we shared—
How each helped make the other's
    dream complete—
The way we laughed about but little
    cared
The tide was in and lapping at our
    feet.

The holiday is past, but even so,
A pleasant memory is always new;
And if fate should be kind, perhaps
    I'll go,
Someday, somewhere, to walk again
    with you.

I'd sent for dreams

Dreamer

Your footsteps fell so softly
That I never was aware
Of how or when, from where you came—
Just one day you were there.

The threads that bound me to you
Were fragile as a web,
Entwining with the pulse and breath
Of my life's flow and ebb.

I didn't hear the footsteps
Or see the threads that bound;
I'd sent for dreams and then was slow
To know when they were found.

Because

Because you looked and let your eyes
Linger for a while
Upon my face, into my eyes,
Perhaps searching for a smile,

I felt your gaze, became aware
Of how I dressed and wore my hair.
I gave the smile right from the start,
Then volunteered to give my heart.

First Love

I'd never dreamed
    before you came
That such love would
    have found me;
I'd never looked
    into your eyes,
Nor felt your arms
    around me.

But since you walked
    into my world
And stole this heart
    of mine,
I only want to be
    your girl
And to be near you
    all the time.

Question

Could it be a time existed
When I didn't know your name
And, without you, still persisted
Laughing, singing—just the same?

Could it be? I only know
You've become so much a part
Of life for me that, should you go,
No song could come from half a heart.

Your faith becomes a strand that blends

Tapestry

Because with patient heart
   you watch me go
To weave a pattern that is
   mine alone,
Not asking nor demanding
   that I show
The threads I use are like
   those of your own,

Your faith becomes a strand
   that blends so well,
Reinforcing every thread
   of mine,
Sometimes I wonder if my
   friends can tell
That you are woven in the
   whole design.

I Married a Fisherman

I married a fisherman, so you see
My husband's not always devoted to me.
As soon as he can get awake,
He heads for a stream or fishing lake.
He dearly loves the old boat docks,
He'd risk his life for his tackle box;
He gets a thrill when he gets a strike,
Be it bluegill, bass or pike.

He's a scout and he's a boater,
He takes fine care of his outboard motor;
He thinks the world of his rod and reel,
As a fishing partner, he's ideal.
For if it's sunny or pours the rain,
He's the faithful sort: he won't complain.

But when the fuel is running low
And fish quit biting an hour ago,
His feet are sore, he needs dry clothes,
How that line got tangled no one knows.
It's getting dark, he's all worn out,
His back is burned without a doubt;
He's nearly starved—then definitely
He'll come dragging home to me.

For Better or Worse

"Come live with me and be my love."
How sweet your sentence sounded!
Well, here I am, since days ago,
Amorously unbounded.

But now at times you think that I'm
Too skinny or too fat;
I go too much or spend too much,
I'm too, too this or that.

And though I claim these faults are mine,
You want me just the same:
Through better I give you the praise,
For worse I take the blame.

Transformation

The pattern of my life was
    so complete
I had not missed your presence
    at my door;
Then came the fateful day our
    eyes would meet,
And days I'd want to see you
    more and more,

Until the pattern changed
    and you became
So woven in the substance,
    I confess,
That former days could never
    be the same,
And I could not endure their
    emptiness.

The twig was shaped to be an upright tree

To My Child
(For Nancy)

There is implanted in the heart of you
So much that is good and sweet and pure,
And although you are yet so young and small,
These traits will grow and through your life endure.

I would that I could cultivate the good
While you are yet dependent on my care,
That weeds of greed and hate will ever find
Your life is filled and has no room to spare;

So that when you choose a path your own,
When dreams might lead you far away from me,
All those who look on you might understand
The twig was shaped to be an upright tree.

Queen of Hearts
(For Rhonda)

I watch you every morning leave for school,
Your hair is brushed, your face all scrubbed and clean;
Your shoes are tied and neat, by ordered rule,
But something strange will happen there between
The time you go and when you come again
With face all smudged, your hair a tangled mess,
Your socks rundown and somehow slightly stained,
And spots where soup has spilled onto your dress.

Perhaps I should remember little girls
Have an inclination all their own
For things like wrinkled clothes and matted curls
And other traits that soon will be outgrown.
But how a grown-up father could become
Like putty in those hands I cannot see;
You'd do no better were you twenty-one
And educated in psychology.

From My Child
(By Rhonda)

If it weren't for you, I wouldn't exist;
Just think of the things I would have missed:
Happy good times and occasional thrills,
Clothes that I like and home-cooked meals.

If it weren't for you being just as you are,
I couldn't have possibly made it this far;
I might have bowlegs, buck-teeth or crossed-eyes
And other afflictions that can't be disguised.

I would lack the poise and self-confidence
That I usually find with the compliments
I see in your eyes when you're not aware
That I'm searching and longing to find them there.

If it weren't for you, I couldn't be me;
As a matter of fact, I'd not even be!
So if words can express gratitude and such
My words are simply, "I love you this much!"

Tomboy

Pretty little girl of ten,
I look at you and wonder when
You will stop your climbing trees
With stubbed-off toes and skinned-up knees.

You sometimes dress in pretty clothes
With ruffles, frills and dainty bows,
But you display a lack of poise
Out shooting marbles with the boys.

One day Cupid's fiery dart
Will make a target of your heart;
Then you'll lose your rugged mood
And feign a helpless attitude.

Letter to Jonathan

Dear Jon,

Perhaps we'd call it my mistake
To say I'd meet you at the lake;
But Pop and David rushed you on,
They just kept saying, "We want Jon
To show us how he got that prize."
(You'd caught a carp three-fourths
     your size.)

I thought you'd settle for the dock
And not go climb that old slick rock,
But having passed your fishing test,
You thought this casting spot was best.

Then when I later reached the boat
To join my angling group afloat,
I saw, instead of sparkling sails,
Wet underwear across the rails;
And just inside the sliding door,
Two soppy shoes lay on the floor.

I nearly skinned your Pop alive
To think he'd let a boy of five
Explore a spot your Nanny fears—
You'd just gone under, head and ears!

Love,

Nanny

Pop's House

Pop's house is a place where now and then
Four grandchildren gather in.
They know their Nanny wants to cook
The things they like, and Pop will look
At football passes David learned
And how Jon's baseball skill has turned,
How Leigh Ann marches with baton
And Candice yells to cheer them on.

When nighttime comes they all will head
Straight for Nanny's king-size bed,
And as four heads lie in a row
With forty toes stuck out below,
She takes them to enchanted lands
Of the storybook held in her hands.

When all too soon the visit ends
(It matters not how long it's been),
Before they leave they want to know,
"Do we really have to go?"
Then Pop and Nanny understand
Why people call such children grand.

For we may have the Christmas star

The Christmas Star

The star that formed the shepherd's
  guiding light
To where a king had come, by humble
  birth,
Has not been banished from the skies
  of night,
But still exists beyond the realm of
  earth.

And we who lift our eyes, prepared
  to go,
With anxious heart, not questioning
  how far,
Find we, like shepherd men, the King
  may know,
For we, as they, may have the
  Christmas star.

One Day

One day God will break
    the silver cord
That now confines me to
    an earthly way,
And who can know the grace
    He will afford
To sweep me to the land
    of endless day?

One day the end of faith
    will be revealed;
I'll see no more as through
    a darkened glass,
For Heaven's glories will
    not be concealed
When through the gates of
    splendor I shall pass.

Wives of Jacob
(Genesis)

Leah was first to wear the name of Jacob,
First to lie beside him in his tent;
Six times she brought to him a son or daughter
To seal the bonds and ties that marriage meant.
And Leah took the care that Jacob gave her,
Knowing she must never put to test
The place he held for her within his heart,
For she knew always he loved Rachel best.

Rachel was her father's second daughter,
Destined to be Jacob's second wife;
And she, who longed so much to hold his children,
Would have a second son to claim her life.
Even death would mean for Leah honor,
A tomb within the family burial ground;
While Rachel's grave, denoted by a marker,
Beside the road to Bethlehem is found.

Across the centuries I read their story
And feel that Rachel understood her fate:
That she could give to Leah all the glory—
She had the greater love to compensate.

My Prayer

Lord, I would ask that You'd help me to climb
To the top of the mountain of faith,
And there let me know, for a sweet space of time,
The thrill of Your shower of grace.

Forgetting the depth of the valley beneath,
To know but the touch of Your hand,
And, too, though I'm human and fail You so much,
You're God—and You still understand.

So then when I find myself starting to doubt
Or to question the faith that is mine,
I'll pause to recall my communion with God
And the strength You have helped me to find.

The Garden

A garden grew eastward in Eden
When earth was but sea and the sod,
And man, from the dust of the ground,
Was made in the image of God.

The garden held all living creatures
And trees that were stately and grand;
There was food that would please and sustain him
And a river to flow through the land.

The man would be joined by a woman,
A wife who would love him and share;
But temptation grew in the garden
That they were not able to bear.

When God sent them out from the garden,
All mankind would share in the fall,
For we have the same human nature;
We, too, would have wanted it all.

But sometimes, when we walk close by Him,
He lets us see Eden in wait,
For God never did move the garden—
He just set a watch at the gate.

Shepherd

The Lord is my shepherd
Through good days and bad;
He knows of the pleasure
And sadness I've had.

The valleys and shadows
Have been very real,
But so have green pastures
And waters so still.

The past and the future
Are held in His care,
For He is the shepherd
And why should I fear?

Somehow my heart knows only that you're gone

First Letter

We knew, of course, you'd
    come to me one day
To say your ship was heading
    out to sea.
We long had known it had to
    be this way;
There'd be no tears for soon
    you'd come to me.

I stood down on the pier and
    watched until,
Obscured by the horizon from
    my view,
Your ship was gone; then,
    lingering still,
I wished a voyage safe and
    speedy, too.

I told myself again about
    the day
You'd come and I'd no longer
    be alone.
And then I wept. No matter
    what I say,
Somehow my heart knows only
    that you're gone.

When I Miss You

If you should want to know when
  I miss you,
I miss you when my cherished
  hopes and plans
Have gone amiss, and when the
  need is new
To have someone who cares and
  understands.

I miss you when the morning sun
  is bright
And fields are glistening with
  the early dew;
I miss you when the day turns
  into night
And life is filled with
  everything but you.

The glow that lights your eyes,
  the gentle touch,
Your voice and all that makes
  you seem so dear,
These are the things I miss so
  very much
Just anytime at all when
  you're not here.

Wayne

Once we knew a golden boy
With sunlight in his hair,
With laughter in his heart and eyes,
Who had a song to share.

His life was marked by special ways,
At home, at school and church the same,
Not measured by the length of days,
But by the brightness of the flame.

Now all too soon the sunlight,
The laughter and the song
Are gone from us, for Wayne abides
In a new and golden home.

Inside the Gate

I wonder if they rang the bells
For him inside the gate,
And if the angels rushed to tell
The many friends who wait.

Were they anxious that he see
The shining jasper wall,
The golden streets, the crystal stream,
The splendor of it all?

Or did they gently bid him rest
Beside a golden stair,
Knowing he would think it best
To wait till we are there?

The Quest We Shared

I had a childhood friend who ran with me
In search of every good and pleasant thing;
We waded streams that flowed out to the sea
And climbed the hills to hear wind whispering.

We looked beyond confinement of our day
To wonder what the cup of life would hold
And pledged that, hand in hand, we'd wend our way
Until we reached the rainbow's flaming gold.

But then she died. I saw life ebb away,
Beheld them as they laid her down to rest.
I sorrowed that we could no longer play
And wept that she could not fulfill her quest.

Without the one with whom I'd shared a dream,
I went to taste the nectar, touch the gold.
I found them not exactly as they seemed—
The gleam we saw but half the story told.

Now having tasted of the cup, I know
It holds some bitterness, some acid stain,
And all who come within the flaming glow
Find, mingled with the beauty, searing pain.

And I, who once shed tears in wasted grief
For all the things that were not meant to be,
Have slowly come to foster the belief
That, could she know, she'd sometimes weep for me.

He'd been my friend

The Old Man's View

He'd been my friend, the old man on the hill,
Though he lived in a solemn atmosphere;
He always seemed so unperturbed until
I asked him if he ever shed a tear.

He said, "It's true, where once I'd laugh or cry,
A smile or frown now indicates my mood;
But I recall so many days when I
Saw all things in a light of magnitude—

The heat so hot, the cold such bitter cold,
My joy or sorrow always so intense;
But now I'm tempered and am growing old
And mountains in my life are less immense.

I seem to see the seasons blend as one,
As colors fuse to form a golden hue;
Perhaps one day, dear child, the time will come
When you'll have such a panoramic view."

Recognition

He rose up early every working day
To sit across the table from his wife;
His work was hard and earned him little pay,
But you could tell he loved their simple life.

Unlike so many in their quest for gain,
He recognized the things he labored for:
His children ran to meet him in the lane,
And she'd always be waiting at the door.

Second Childhood

When he was young he must
    have been compelled
To carry water, chop the
    wood all day;
His many chores must surely
    have withheld
More time than he could ever
    find to play.

And now in later years his
    work is done
So quickly that it seems to
    be a joy;
Not quick because he finds
    his work is fun,
But so there's time to be a
    little boy.

Teacher's Retirement

How many times in all the years
Have bells and buzzers rung?
How many children walked the halls?
How many anthems sung?

How many classroom sessions spent
With lessons to be learned
Before the students came to claim
Diplomas they had earned?

How many friendships have been made
And proven worth the knowing?
Well, just enough to fill a life
And heart to overflowing.

Committee Chairman

They named him chairman for the latest project,
One of high improbability.
For days and weeks he worked, defying logic,
And any help was more than I could see.

Then proud and pleased when next came time to meet,
He was a study in pure self-control,
Except I faintly heard him grit his teeth
While someone told how "we" had reached the goal.

And men still long for Edens that are lost

After Eden

Eden was not seen as Paradise
So long as something more remained in doubt.
Desire that promised to anoint the eyes
Became a curse that drove the tenants out.

And ever after some have sought to build
Designs into a garden. Knowing not the cost,
They cultivate forbidden trees to yield—
And men still long for Edens that are lost.

Once Again

So many days had passed
    since you were here
That I'd forgotten how
    your eyes could shine,
The funny little smile
    that would appear
Each time your glance would
    coincide with mine.

But now you come again
    reminding me
How nice it was, how long
    the time has been,
And though it brings a
    pleasant memory,
I know I should forget you
    once again.

Half-Truth

They said one day you'd go away from me,
Forgetting we had ever met at all;
They wanted me to know lest I should be
Shocked and disappointed by the fall.

You went away just as they said you would—
The flame that burned is nothing but an ember.
They think how their prediction was so good,
Not knowing all the times you will remember.

Dear Prince

They told me all
      the things you were—
Charming, handsome,
      debonair.

They said you had
      a line so sweet
It swept a girl
      right off her feet,
And that no matter
      where you went
No lonely hour
      was ever spent.

They didn't tell me
      that your eyes
Were soft and kind,
      your manner wise,
Nor that your witty,
      pleasant way
Could brighten up
      just any day.

I learned this for
      myself, you know;
I wish they'd told me
      . . . years ago.

The Flame That Burned

One night, across a crowded room,
You looked at me, and I at you;
There was no word, no lilting tune,
Yet from the spark a small flame grew.

We met again on other nights;
I grew accustomed to your name.
Your presence, music, candlelight,
All combined to fan the flame.

And then you went your separate way,
Knowing there'd be no return,
For we remember how one day
The rains fell on the flame that burned.

Observations

Easy Does It!

I can rise to face the dawn
With fortitude unless
A shattering alarm should rouse
Me from my sleepiness.

To be thus awakened
Unnerves me for the day,
And no amount of peace and quiet
Can undo the fray.

So if you'd have me cheerful
(It won't happen accidently) ,
Just turn the radio on low
And wake me up real gently.

Observation

When, in public, couples are
Simply man and wife,
Their reservations indicate
They have a blissful private life.

But if they call each other
Darling, in sweet tones,
It's just an act to camouflage
The fights they have at home.

Doctor to Patient

You say you read
    or toss and turn
And try such things
    as counting sheep;
In spite of all,
    you reaffirm,
You simply cannot
    go to sleep.

Well, tired and worn,
    I'd like to see
Some twist of fate
    or circumstance
Give you my sleeping
    tendency
Or me your wasted
    chance.

For Heaven's Sake!

His daughter dressed in old blue jeans
And wondered if he'd care;
With lashes curled and eyelids green,
She wore a blond rinse on her hair.

Although she feared what he might say,
He didn't make a fuss;
But when at night he knelt to pray,
She heard him ask, "Deliver us!"

About-Face

He always knew the answers to
The TV contest flings;
His comment, when contestants missed,
Was something like, "You stupid things!"

But once they asked him to partake
And he was not the same;
He missed his chance to win the stake—
He didn't even know his name.

To stand beside the summit evergreens

The Challenge

I did not choose to climb the highest hill,
And yet the one I set my mark upon
Withstood itself against my stubborn will,
As if to thwart my plans for going on.

But slowly, step by step, I inched my way
Over cliffs, around the deep ravines,
Until I came at last, through heat of day,
To stand beside the summit evergreens.

I looked in triumph down the tangled path
By which I'd made my slow ascent until
I knew I had the strength and will to match
The challenge of this rugged, daring hill.

This Day for Me

Another day has dawned for me,
How bright the rising sun!
Somehow I feel that it will be
Unlike no other one.

So as the hours and moments pass,
And as the day unfolds,
I'll be awaiting, anxiously,
The promise that it holds.

The Gentle Brook

I walked today down by a gentle brook
To watch the current as it hurried by.
The surface, ever moving as I looked,
Was calm and smooth, reflecting earth and sky.

I heard a pleasant ripple here and there
Where objects loomed, as if defiantly;
The volume moving on, I knew not where,
Replenished by a source I could not see.

Beyond this point, I know, the water slows
To shallow pool that makes no sound at all,
And farther on again it churns and flows
Down precipice into a waterfall.

How strange it was to think this gentle stream
Could know such change as comes to even me—
With shallow spots and waterfalls that gleam,
When brook was really all it meant to be.

To My Friend

The journey had been difficult
And winds had chilled me through;
My body ached with hunger
When I encountered you.

You built a fire to warm me
And shared with me your bread,
You recognized my need and gave
A pillow for my head.

And now when others talk about
The way some friendships grow
Or how a friend can warm the heart,
I answer, "Yes . . . I know."

The Mountain Top

The mountain top has been for me
Symbol of a happy place;
The wildest flowers are here to see,
And soft winds blow across your face.

Squirrels go darting through the trees
And, on the first plateau,
You see small birds and rabbits feed
Where possum grapes and berries grow.

The nicest sounds are often heard
Here on this lofty hill—
The sassy song of mockingbird,
The slow, sure chant of whippoorwill.

In contrast to the town below,
With all its hurried, hectic pace,
These sights and sounds are good to know—
This hill is such a peaceful place.